I0469536

ISBN-13: 978-1481989114

ISBN-10: 1481989111

Table of Contents

Teeing It Up

With a sport or game we embrace the need for practice, the helpfulness of a coach and even the inevitable pre-performance nerves. We are here to suggest that adopting a similar attitude adjustment for presentations will help you knock it out of the park.

Giving a presentation. Sharing a keynote. Leading a meeting. Facilitating a webinar. Each is a game, and you are the player. As with a game, the equipment and uniforms are expected. Rules are known and sometimes challenged. Opponents are assumed expected and welcomed. There are skills to learn and, most importantly, an attitude to adopt.

For our purposes, the term *presentation* will be used to represent all the different forms of verbal and/or visual communication including keynotes, phone conferences, phone calls, webinars, meetings, pitches, proposals, reports, interviews, etc. If your presentation is a game, then you are in it to win.

Sports and presenting have many things in common. As teachers we have relied on the universality of sports references for helping to explain many concepts. Most of us at some point, from childhood into adulthood, have been a player, a coach, or a fan, and we understand the play of a game. With a little shift of perspective, we get our head in the game and can experience the attitude adjustment needed to move from work to play, head to body, and "what should I do?" to "I know this."

We expect players to have different levels of skill, and we know that tips, techniques, practice and coaching can help them improve. While some players are naturally skilled, others just love to play the game, and still others are roped in, promoted in, or just filling in. Regardless of whether the player is in the minor league, the major league, or even the pros, skills are continually being honed. Why then, in presentations, do we often feel we should be able to perform at a high level without practice?

For example, many of us would approach a long walk with the attitude: "I mean really, how hard can it be? I exercise all the time." But for anyone who has done a day-long walk or hike, you know that a full day of walking does indeed use different muscles from jogging or biking, and we are reminded of this when we are found hobbling at the end of the 34-mile event. However, those who prepare with something as simple as training in distance walking stroll on past the others and keep walking the next day. Public speaking often presents us with a

similar feeling: "Shouldn't I be fairly decent at this? I speak all the time." We suit up; we show up, and think that we should be fine. We assume that we can wing it, but presenting uses different muscles and skills. Practice does make a difference. And being coached does improve your game. Ask any athlete.

In addition, when we have been away from the game for a while, the expectations, personal skills, even equipment and playing fields may have changed. If you were a high school or college athlete and a friend asks for a pickup game, you might say, "Oh, I played in high school, it will come back to me." And while some of that is thankfully true, we also have older bodies, along with some bad habits stored in our muscle memory. It is worth doing a little stretch, a warm-up, and practice so that we are ready to compete again and, as in both games and presentations, to go for our goal.

www.skillbites.net

The Game

Isn't this why we are here: to play, to have fun, and ultimately, to win? The game is any communication that we have with anyone. The game may be scheduled, or it could be impromptu, but whenever it happens, we need to be prepared to play.

In order to prepare for the game, once we know the goal, we need to assess the roles and implications of the separate components: the playing field, the players, the rules. Each one of these aspects affects our game and the plays we choose, and the more we are aware of them, the more prepared we will be to show up ready.

As football great Joe Madden said, "Failure to prepare is to prepare to fail."

The Goal

Games by definition have goals. Often it is to win by obtaining a certain score. Or sometimes the goal of the game is simply to have fun. While some people enjoy the competitive energy, some are more drawn to the play. Each and every presentation, or moment of communication, has a goal or objective. Being clear about your goal affects the level of your play. Clearer the objective, the more committed the action and thus more effective the delivery.

Be very specific on what you want the intended audience to take away from your presentation. Be clear on lining up both what you think they are expecting and what you are intending. Remember: it is more important to provide them with what they need to hear than what you want to say.

Overall, clear communication, with a resulting action from the audience, is what we hope to achieve. But that response can take many different forms. It can be the yes to a deal; it can be the sell; it can be the empowerment of the knowledge shared; it can be the "ah ha" of guiding to self-discovery. We could be seeking visibility/exposure, or seeking new customers.

We must prepare by asking a variety of questions to lead us to our specific goal. Why are you doing this particular presentation or leading this meeting? Why am I the one presenting and not someone else? Why at this time? What do they need? What are the expectations?

As in a game, once the goal is identified, the presenter needs to assess the situation, plan out, and execute game tactics. Those tactics are the various ways in which you intend to reach your audience. Those tactics are The Play of the Game. That's when it can get really fun and your own unique spin emerges.

The Playing Field

We realize the playing field is different for each sport. We know that surfaces and dimensions vary and that this impacts the game. We know it matters whether a game is being played on artificial turf or on natural grass. Such differences matter in a presentation as well. Delivery and impact vary depending on the situation. A presentation in a boardroom is vastly different from a keynote given in an auditorium, and completely different from a phone conference in a meeting room. But it is also important to assess the subtle differences between board and meeting rooms; between different auditoriums; or, between different web platforms.

Here are a number of questions to get you started: are you on a conference call and do you have to stay within the confines of the table or training room? Or can you take it elsewhere? Where are you in relation to the speaker and the microphone?

Is there video to watch? How many people are listening and from where are they listening? Are there different languages and time zones?

Are you offering a webinar? Are they seeing a PowerPoint? Who is running the webinar? How many people are watching/listening? How long is the webinar?

Is there a moderator? Are you on a headset or are you using your computer's microphone? Do you have a backup if one connection goes out?

Are you at a lectern? At a podium? Where is it positioned: right, left or center? Is it a solid lectern? What height?

Is there a stage? If you are on stage, where is the light? Can you move and still stay lit? Where is the best light? Where is the strongest position from which to present in this particular space?

Is it a meeting room? How is the lighting? Does the sound bleed from nearby rooms?

Where are you in relationship to the screen - if there is one? Is there more than one screen?

Are you mic'd? If so, what kind of microphone are you using? Should you wear a particular type of shirt or suit for the microphone?

How are the seats laid out? Where will people be seated? Will the seats be full? Are they all facing you? Are the people seated at tables or in rows?

How large is the space? What is the room shape? Where are you in relation to the door?

Are there windows to the outside? Are you back-lit? Will the light from the windows affect how well people can see you, or how well you can see them? Can you close the blinds? Are there windows to the rest of the office or area? Can people see in?

Are you having a job interview? In whose office? How are the seats arranged? Is there a desk or a table? How many people are present? What is your position in relation to door and to interviewer?

All of these details, and many more, define the playing field. Often presenters neglect to consider the impact of their environment on their presentation and are thrown by it during the actual process. How one adjusts and responds to each of these variables is part of the game tactics. This will reduce the number of surprises.

If you have considered all of these variables before going out onto the field, you will be better prepared to excel – taking advantage of the unique quality of each venue.

The Player

We have only ourselves to bring to the game. We are the player. We must know and capitalize on our strengths and talents. Our style of play depends greatly on our own unique physique and personality….the same with presenting. Have we trained and practiced? Do we know what works for us?

The verbal and non-verbal elements of our communication have equally important impact on our audience.

The presenter's speaking voice is a tool often overlooked. We acknowledge we prefer some voices to others, but often we do not realize that elements of our own voice are under our control.

And it is something we should consider since the audience decides a great deal about the presenter, the information, and the presenter's knowledge of the topic based on vocal qualities. A pitcher works on the pitching form, the swimmer on the stroke – they focus on the key element of their sport. Why would it be any different with a presenter and her/his voice? Yet, many people have never considered the impact of their voice. If we are on the phone or webinar, our voice becomes even more important because the listeners are assuming and filling in the visual blanks based on our voices.

Your voice is part of your package as a presenter, and will be given a more in depth discussion in a further book.

You can get a free assessment of your speaking voice and presentation style by requesting it at www.ARTiculateRC.com.

Our non-verbal communication is "heard" loud and strong. That does not mean it is always heard as we assume, and that is why we must be aware of the messages being conveyed. The list of non-verbal elements is endless. Absolutely everything about our being, that is not our voice, is part of our non-verbal communication. This includes our clothes, shoes, hair, age, ethnicity, kempt or unkempt appearance, and so on. People read physical comfort or discomfort in how we enter the room. We are communicating constantly through how we carry ourselves, our eye contact, how close or far we stand, how strong or loose our handshake is, how we sit, and so on.

We need to know ourselves well enough that we are aware and possibly can monitor how we are communicating using both our physical message and our vocal message while we are speaking.

X's and O's

Tactics move us toward our goal. The tactics are the x's and o's of the football plan. These are the chosen speeds and angles for the ski run. These are the choices available to make your presentation most effective. They include message detail and text flow, use of your voice and body, incorporation of audio and visual effects and more. These elements dictate the impact of the play.

The presenter may mistakenly think that to simply express the words connected to a thought or an idea is clear communication, as if they can toss out a ball in a haphazard manner, leaving it up to the other player to either catch or return it. Note: It takes both parties to engage in a game. It takes both parties to complete the communication. Without the other, there is no game nor does communication take place. Without the other it is simply practice or dropping off of an errand.

By definition tactics means that we are trying a variety of means to an end. Rarely does the presenter communicate a full message that an audience fully understands on the first attempt. This highlights why we must utilize different means to get our message across. In sports we understand that those tactics of moving the football make it exciting. When the quarterback and wide receiver click – a thing of beauty occurs, but there are other attempts that don't. Being open to assessing failed attempts and to trying a variety of options enhances the presentation and the connection to the audience.

There is a give and take between the presenter and the audience, whether the presenter is delivering a keynote or a webinar. On this playing field, the presenter may or may not be able to audibly hear or physically see the responses of the audience, and this may make them think that communication is a one-way street; however, the best presentations occur as dialogues. Same in a sport -- a team may practice alone, but the game involves another team.

Every player must step up and play. Don't *talk* about playing – start the game. Don't *talk* about what you are going to talk about, dive in.   Our fellow players and audience members have shown up, and you must engage them at the outset. You do not have to tell them where you are going to go – just start going and trust they will follow. You have a limited time to catch the attention of the audience so don't waste it telling them what you are going to be telling them anyway.

Can you challenge the norm by doing something different, or change the culture? Do you want to?

Possible questions to ask: Is it a come and go meeting and/or presentation, or will they be a captive audience? Did they choose to be there, or was it chosen for them?

How much time do you have? Can you keep track? Is there a clock you can see? Do you keep a watch handy for this purpose? Can someone watch it and alert you?

The Rules

In sports, established rules govern the game. When a rule is broken, the game is stopped, the error pointed out and some adjustment made, and play resumes. It seems fairly objective. In the world of presentations, rules are mostly subjective, and this can cause hesitation in play. There are some rules that are objective – e.g., the amount of time for the presentation and the topic, but many rules are subjective.

Rules are what keep us within certain bounds of play. We know what we can or cannot do. Ironically, it gives us freedom to play. Without these guidelines, the game may feel out of control. Or we may be restricted by fear of doing it "wrong," without knowing specifically what "wrong" is.

16

Pause and check when you hear yourself say, "I can't do that." Be aware of the rulebook you are following. Some are helpful rules; some are assumed rules; and some rules no longer apply.

Good Plays

It would be helpful to know what many people deem to be good plays and/or tactics and are in line with our objective of clear communication. So what are those good plays? How do we know which to employ?

On the following page is a list of presentation elements that fellow presenters have defined as helping make a presentation effective. They are subjective. But the list reminds us that as presenters, and as an audience, we know what works for us.

Articulation

Audience interaction

Believable

Breathe

Clarity

Clear story

Confidence

Connection

Conversational tone

Crispness

Direction – "objective"

Energy

Emotionally engaged

Engaging

Enthusiasm for subject and audience

Environment

Expressiveness

Eye contact

Flexibility – impromptu changes

Flow – physically and information

Grounded - relaxed

Hands

Humility

Humor – natural

Intention – objective

Intentional pauses

Interactive

Interesting topic

Just the right amount of hand gesture

Know audience

Know own style

Knowledge of the subject

Movement connected

Openness – vulnerability

Passion

Pauses

Physical appearance

Posture and confidence

Prosody – rhythm and sound of
   the voice

Real

Repetition

Respect

Sincerity

Smile

Spontaneity

Stories

Strong voice

Succinct

"Take aways" for audience

True connection

Trust

Variety of pacing

Visual aids

Vocal variation

Vocally connected

Word choice appropriate

A Few Key Rules

The pause vs. the um: Learn to rely on and believe in the power of the pause. The pause honors your audience. It gives them a fraction of a moment to think about and process what you have shared. It frames the thoughts you are expressing. It is exhausting for your audience to edit out the filler words and um's that can litter verbal communication while they try to find the core message. The filler words are spam in the inbox. They are verbal static that muddies the message. Trust the pause.

Objective: As in mountain biking or skiing, we need to see our line and hold to it. If I look at the rock I don't want to hit, I will often go right into it. Presenting is the same. Know your objective, see it and go for it. Keep your attention on what you are sharing and giving to them. If you start thinking about yourself and whether or not you are doing an "ok" job, or if you are focusing on one person who does not seem to be paying attention, you will lose sight of your objective – and ultimately, crash into the rock. This blurred focus may create a loss of confidence or loss of thought. Know your line and stick to it.

Nerves: Reframe any known nervousness as excitement. You are about to play, and your heart races, your palms sweat, you may have to run to the restroom. In sports, it is known as

excitement – anticipation to play hard and do a good job. In presenting, reframe the same physiological reactions as excitement and play to win. Presence of nerves indicate that you actually care. They are good sign. Make friends with them – use them. Don't fall prey to assuming you are scared to speak in pubic when you might just be nervous. You might actually enjoy it and that is not an admittance that you are an attention seeker, but simply someone who enjoys sharing information or ideas with others.

Breathe! Get in your athlete's body and connect with that breath. The presenter breath is often high and shallow. When we are practicing whatever sport we play, our breath drops low and deep. Present from there. Use that breath. More on this in Book II.

Fouls and Errors

When do our choices on presentation style actually sacrifice or obstruct our main goal of clear communication? For instance, have you ever given a presentation during which you knew that you had lost your audience but did not know why? Or perhaps, as an audience member, you walked away without understanding what had been shared in the presentation? Just as in sports, sometimes the foul is obvious and you know just what you did to get the whistle blown. But often we don't know when we created a foul while presenting. In sports we may ask: what am I doing that is slowing my time, messing up my swing, or actually hurting my body? In presenting, what are the common fouls that cause me to miss my goal?

Language can create barriers in understanding. Use of jargon, specific words and phrases, is essential within an industry or group. But when presenting to a mixed or outside audience, be very careful of the alienation or distance created with the use of jargon. You want to hold your audience's attention, and any word that causes a pause of misunderstanding is a moment you lose them.

Additionally, when language is used that causes the audience to mentally leave your presentation in order to figure out what you either said or what you are talking about, a foul has occurred. We need to be aware of the terms, stats, data, and phrases that we are choosing to use with our audience.

A presenter wants to keep the audience with them on the journey, and when the audience is trying to figure out what was either said or meant, they have missed your next point. Note that this is different from entertainment such as in a novel, a film or in storytelling where we like to try to figure out what is going on and what might happen next. In presentations, it is often more effective to give the "bang" first and then explain how you got there.

Everyone: Presenters need to be aware of using universal language such as "all" or "everyone". For example, "Everyone knows this or that." Even if 99% of the group does, this type of inclusivity can cause the 7th grader that lurks in many of us to surface and rebel. Members of the audience can be distracted and start to disengage because they are in their heads thinking, "Not me."

Word Choice: In speech, a presenter may attempt to demonstrate their intellectual prowess by using a lexicon that is elevated and seemingly highly erudite. The prior sentence is a great example. This can be a major foul for the audience. Authenticity is key, and is more effective when using vocabulary that is our own, allowing us to be comfortable and natural, thus making it easier for the audience to follow the information and connect. When speakers attempt to access language that is not as familiar to their everyday vocabulary, they create a foul, most times, by creating malapropisms* and a stiffness to their delivery. Be real, be yourself. You are enough. Actually, you are more than enough if you really show up!

Reading: A pervasive foul is when presenters read or memorize a presentation, word for word, which can create a stilted delivery. It often does not leave space for dialogue, the give and take between the presenter and the listener. In sports, it would mean we would perform memorized moves and then use them in a game without taking into account variables of the other players. The same principle functions in presentation. The presenter, ultimately, desires to communicate a message. In order for that to happen, the presenter needs to create space for the audience to process what is being shared and allow them time to provide their response. Warning: sometimes people are more engaged than they appear. Checking a watch or a yawn does not mean they are not engaged. They may be worried about a babysitter, or they may have been up late the night before.

Another fallout of memorizing a presentation is that it "sounds" read which usually does not engage your audience, and can largely be attributed to the fact that we write differently than we speak. Playwrights, film and TV writers know this – they are highly skilled at capturing the way we speak. A beautifully written speech must take into account that it will be shared aloud. In presentations, we need to remember that we speak in chunks. We don't usually speak in full sentences. We are fully aware of this in every day communication. It is only when we feel the pressure of a heightened presentation that we make choices against our instincts as if it is a more professional choice. Allowing our natural communication style to guide us will connect us to our audience more effectively, and in the end, allow for a professional and more meaningful connection.

Some helpful tools for preparation and memorization are:

- Narrow down the speech or presentation to bullet points and then practice speaking to the bullet points, which means that the material needs to be known really, really well.
- Lay it out as a mind map instead of a linear outline.
- Use color to designate different points
- Write and rewrite your talking points.
- Practice it out loud in the car, in the shower, while distracted and let it be different and evolving.
- Get it into your muscle memory; get it into your body.

Hands: A player's hands are also important to the game. It matters how we hold a golf club, a baseball bat; how the catcher's glove is positioned when a pitch is crossing home plate. In presentations, our hands guide our thought process, and they need to be kept in the game. We also want to keep physically open to our audience and not use our hands to

close off. Often presenters do not feel comfortable with their hands because they have heard they should avoid using them or that they use them too much. If a presenter attempts to harness them or subvert them, the presenter may have trouble with their train of thought. Many of us use our hands when we speak on the phone. Voice Over artists/actors use their hands when recording a script even though no one can see them. Our hands help us organize our thoughts. In presentations, our hands also help the listener/watcher, follow our train of thought as well. When choosing to use them, let them compliment the words, clarify and enhance the message.

A few common errors occur when we don't let our hands enhance our speaking. Arms can get stuck in "presentation position", bent at elbow and not being used. The hands can get locked into "spiders on the mirror", the "steeple", the "clasp", etc. Repetitive parallel gestures, like the ones given by the person on the tarmac, trying to direct the plane into the gate, are not connected to meaning. And an attempt to keep the hands calm and non-expressive can become the "inmate or the fig leaf" position, hands clasped behind the back of the body or in front of the zipper.

Moving: Movement during a presentation is the same as with the hands. If it is connected to the message and the audience, it works. If it is simply just pacing or locked in place, it muddies or confuses the communication.

Habits: As presenters, we need to be aware of our own presentation and speaking habits. When we are aware of our habits, we can learn to play with them. If we try to squelch them, they will just reappear as something else. I can remember learning my swing in golf. When I tried to correct my swing, so that I wouldn't slice the ball, my bad habit reappeared as a shank. A little like whack a mole -- you suppress one bad habit, and another pops up. In presentations, our bad habits may include saying um, speaking quickly, holding our hands a certain way or pacing. We don't intend to perform badly in a game or competition or to have habits that create bad communication. When a player can make a note of the habits that aren't working in their game, they can learn new habits. When our habits surface, we can use them as a signal to pay attention to what must be happening inside ourselves as presenters, make an adjustment and our game will improve. And remember, our habits were created for a reason. Don't punish yourself for them. Just examine them and see if they still serve a purpose. These are a few of the fouls that can occur during the play of the game. Often, we are unaware of our own habits. In order to become familiar with them, it helps to be filmed or have a trusted friend watch our presentation and share their observation. Coaching and/or a professional group, such as Toastmasters, can provide the needed practice and consistent feedback.

Contact us for a free assessment and suggestions: www.ARTiculateRC.com

Practice

Preparation, practice, rehearsal - call it what you will, the presenter needs it as much as the athlete. Our audience deserves a presenter that has prepared and has a well-rehearsed game plan. It can be downright annoying if it is obvious that a presenter did not prepare. In sports, a player would be off the team if they did not show up to practice and then showed up on game day unprepared. Practicing and refining our technique are essential so that we can perform at the top of our game while under pressure.

Because we cannot take a lesson and incorporate it immediately into our next competition, a presenter needs to practice in a safe environment so that the new concepts and skills become familiar and second nature. After practicing, a presenter can use those higher, newly acquired skills when needed most - without having to think about it.

We know many of the skills to work on. We even agree with many of them, and yet, often we find that we do not follow them. We may appreciate expressiveness and vocal variation, but we may find that it does not work for us; it feels uncomfortable; or it may feel less than professional. Just as in sports, we watch professional athletes try new techniques that accelerate their play, but these same techniques may be foreign to us. We may feel funny trying them. It will take practice, classes, and sometimes an individual coach, to lift us to a new level of play. Increasing your skill level and learning new moves is essential for clear communication and ultimately, for career advancement.

There is art in good play. There is art in the excellent use of skills.

With just a little attitude adjustment, you can focus on the goal and go play – to win.

Coming Soon

(Spring 2013) FURTHERING THE PLAYS SO YOU CAN PLAY FARTHER (BOOK II)

About the Authors

Hilary Blair is a presentation and speaking voice specialist. She is also a professional voice-over artist and actor with over 30 years' experience teaching, coaching and facilitating. She teaches speaking voice, public speaking with ARTiculate: Real&Clear and is on faculty at the Denver Center for the Performing Arts and adjunct faculty at a number of local colleges and universities. She is a highly regarded coach working extensively across the US at a variety of schools, universities, arts centers, theaters and in corporate settings with actors and teachers to lawyers and CEO's. She holds an MFA from the National Theatre Conservatory and a BA from Yale University. She is a member of Toastmasters and VASTA – the voice and speech trainers association. Hilary is honored to have worked with finalists and awardees of the Make Mine a Million $ Business program since its inception. Hilary enjoys golfing, cycling, mountain biking, and Boggle.

Robin A. Miller, PhD, MDiv is the co-founder of ARTiculate: Real&Clear, a communication and presentation company that helps individuals clarify their message. She is an energetic, motivational keynote speaker and has spent over 20 years in teaching, training and coaching. Robin earned her PhD from the University of North Texas in Musicology and her Master of Divinity from Iliff School of Theology. She has taught at Baylor University, Texas Christian University, and worked as a Customer Relationship Manager in the financial industry, as well as a Development Specialist in some of Denver's leading Level 1 trauma centers. Her background in teaching, vocal performance, and public speaking enables her to work with large groups in actualizing their communication skills by connecting them to the real meaning of their message. She loves sports, spending many years playing competitive fast pitch softball.

Contact Us OnLine:

http://www.articulaterc.com

FaceBook: http://www.facebook.com/ArticulateRealClear

www.ingramcontent.com/pod-product-compliance
Lightning Source LLC
Chambersburg PA
CBHW051420170526
45165CB00004BA/1894